Poetry of a Wanna-Be

Sarah Driscoll

BookLeaf Publishing

India | USA | UK

Presentation by *BookLeaf Publishing*

Web: www.bookleafpub.com

E-mail: info@bookleafpub.com

ISBN: 9789360946524

First edition 2024

*Dedicated to those of us who don't know
what the hell is going on anymore.*

PREFACE

This is purely a form of expression, not a literary work of art. So judge with the heart, not the mind.

Entanglement

A billion years ago we were the same star
But the universe had to expand and condense
This has to be the case
Because it's the only thing that makes sense

Because the laws of quantum mechanics
(If you have ever given them a start)
Describe the very relationship
That our atoms take part

Our atoms stretched far and wide
Across the galaxy and the universe
And it seemed like what once was the same
Would never come to what it was first

But by an act of divine intervention,
Or a series of events one right after another
Our atoms that seemed destined to be apart
Had once again found each other

And when you think of such a miniscule chance
That a star that burned out after a billion years
Isn't the fact that it found its way back together,
A sign that maybe there's more to life than it
appears?

What We Say

Sometimes I feel like you want to say something
And sometimes I do too
So I'm going to take the initiative
And be the first to try and get through

So here I am saying it all
I don't know how it might seem
And I'm telling you now, it feels pretty good
To actually say what I mean

I'm tired of letting our words
Go filtered and guarded all day
Because I want us to finally mean
What we say

Relationships

3

The levels of intimacy we have for each other
Though I'm not sure how it looks
I like to think that our relationship
Goes beyond those in textbooks

I've talked about symbiosis
And feeling like a mother
But that just doesn't quite describe
This relationship we have with each other

I'm sorry if I can't describe
Exactly how I feel
But no matter what happens with us
Know my love for you is real

About You (Just in General)

There's something about you
That I just can't place
But you have completely turned my life around
And I'm grateful in every way

And I'm pretty sure it's obvious
I think these poems are enough proof
That even if you don't want to believe it
I absolutely adore you

And like I've said before
I can't explain why it is this way
But my affection towards you
Only increases by the day

There doesn't always need to be a reason
This is something you'll come to find
Sometimes people will just adore you
And you'll find this more with time

You're an incredibly wonderful person
And you're going to have many people in your
life
Who may end up meaning more to you than me
And that's completely fine

Because you mean a lot to me
And I wish there were more ways to tell you
You bring people comfort
And it's something I wish to do too

There are lots of things that will change in life
And we don't know what will happen as of yet
But I just want to keep reminding you
That I'm very glad we met

Because if we think of the infinite realities
That we could have possibly been put into
Isn't it amazing that I get to live
In the one where I met you?

In the Most Terrible way

You and I are so alike
It's frightening, in a way
That such two people, like ourselves
Should be the ones to play

The parts we play, in this game
Of life, or so I'm told
Feels like some awful trick
And the games are getting old

And just the same, we play this game
Because that's what we're meant to do
But just like how you mean the world
I don't know what I would do without you

You and I are so alike
It's frightening in a way
That when you tell me your troubles
It feels like I'm repeating a day

A day that I'm remembering
Not very unlike yours
The very ones I've once experienced
That had started many wars

But through these wars I've learned to grow
And I want you to do the same
Because like you, I've done it before
So remember, it's all just a game

You and I are so alike
It's frightening in a way
That through me trying to comfort you
You seem to do the same

The way you talk and the way you joke
Like pictures on my shelf
That even through this self-loathing
You've made me learn to like myself

So even though we're so similar
In the battles we fight each day
I think to myself I'm so grateful for it
In the most terrible way

Our Meaning

Don't watch your life pass you by
And yes, right now it's happening
And we don't have enough time
To sit and figure out our meaning

When things are awful
We tend to look for something better and wonder
"when?"
And we forget to pay attention to the good
things
That are happening between now and then

Sometimes it really is worth it
To stop and smell the flowers
We won't experience this again
So don't worry about the hours

And maybe we don't quite know
What our meaning is yet
But there's nothing that says we have to know
now
         Or tomorrow
Or in a year
Or a decade
Or ever
Don't forget

Harness-Training

I told you I'm getting a cat
And I want to harness-train it
Because my apartment is way too small
And cats look better sun-lit

I wouldn't want to get a cat
And keep it trapped inside, under cover
When there's an entire world out there
Just waiting to be discovered

And when you think really hard
About harness-training a cat
It seems really strange in nature
But there's more beyond my doormat

And I want you to remember, if you ever find
yourself
Harness-training a pet
That like inside being too small for a cat
There's more for you than what you'll let

If you ever decide you want more in life
But your fears are what keep reigning
Don't be discouraged by how small it all feels
Maybe you just need some harness-training

Occam's Razor

Have you ever heard of Occam's Razor?
It's an interesting perspective to live by
The simplest explanation for anything
Is usually the one that is right

It's a philosophy partnered with reductionism
In which you'll come to find
Reduces down even the most complex processes
Into ideas easy for the mind

With Occam's Razor you never have to worry
About having to understand anything completely
Because when everything is reduced down into
one thing
Your ignorance is displayed discreetly

I'm not sure if my sarcasm
Is being communicated through
Occam's razor is not the perspective
On life you should choose

Because life as we know it is so complex
There's many things needed to understand
The things that matter most
Are what we need to experience first-hand

There will be things in life in which we do not
like
We'll want to understand in the simplest way
But choosing to minimize its significance
You'll be putting it off for another day

Occam's Razor is comfortable
And easy to digest
When the easiest explanations
are determined to be the best

But when you think of your own problems
And difficulties in life
Was the easiest solution
Really the best one to go by?

The choices we make in life
Will not always be the easiest ones to make
But everything happens for a reason
I promise you

Please wait

Dancing in the Rain

This poem will be a happy one
This one I promise
Because there are so many good things in life
And I feel we should be honest

I should be happy about the rain
And the frost on my car
Because while it feels like an inconvenience
They make what we are

I hate freezer burnt ice-cream
And when my card declines
I hate when I made plans
But would rather stay inside

I hate when my candle wax
Doesn't melt, no good reason
I hate when my nose gets stuffed up
During the change of the season

It all comes down to relativity
What is happy, sad, or real
If we didn't have things that upset us
We wouldn't really know how to feel
"You can't have a rainbow without the rain"

And all of that stuff
Just try to remember there are good things here
When life starts to get rough

I want to learn to appreciate things
And be grateful for things in life
And I think the best way to do that
Is to appreciate the things we don't like

So I'm glad to have rotting food in my fridge
Loud neighbors, bad dogs, no friends
I'm glad I get to experience it
This will not be the end

This life is so mysterious
And pitiful in a way
I want to have good memories
Amongst the bad ones I have today

Nothing

There's nothing in my head right now
Just static with no sound
I don't know what to do with this thought
The fact that there's none around

I go about my day
Pretending I have a thought
But in reality I've lost touch with it
If you are here, then I am not

I think about my room
And how I'm afraid of something
But how does this paranoia
Have anything to do with nothing?

I've cried all of my tears away
My frustrations are a blur
If all I have is nothing
Then I need to be sure

How can I write about nothing
When I have all of this to show
Maybe writing about nothing
Has given me more than I know

My Eyes Are Bleeding

My eyes are bleeding
This much I know
And for everything else
My fears for them grow

"Why can't you stop?"
"Aren't you sad that he's dead?"
"What do you think this is?"
"It's all in your head"

But my eyes are bleeding
Can't anyone see?
My tears are red
And they're drowning me

I sleep on the floor
Someone messed with my meds
There's something in my closet
I don't know what you said

But I do know one thing
while eyes are glistening
I scream in my head
In case anyone is listening

I don't know how to talk
In a way that matters
If it's me or you
I'll always pick the latter

 And I can't really say
That I know for sure
What it is that I want,
Who I am anymore

Because my eyes are bleeding
This much I know
I don't know what I think
What is there in my core

And when I think about
 My troubles each day
Why can't I be grateful?
Just make it go away

I've manifested these problems
"Just stop" you had said
I'm sorry, I didn't mean to
What's wrong with my head?

I'll listen next time

I'll be good I swear
I'll sleep in my bed
I'll stop pulling my hair

My eyes will stop bleeding
If I listen to what you say
But it's been 15 years
And nothing has changed

But what choice do I have?
Nothing else has worked
And though you don't understand
Trying wouldn't hurt

So my eyes are bleeding
So what? Who cares?
"There are people in this world
Who have it worse than you there"

So my eyes have stopped bleeding
Or so you have said
Now I drift off to sleep
While my pillows stain red

No Time

I woke up at 9:30 today
And began to weep alone
I work at 4 o' clock today
And barely have time to clean my home

Because 9:30 is really 10
And 10 is really 12
I haven't eaten a single thing yet
I can't put my books on their shelves

I left that mess from yesterday
But 12 is basically 2
I have no time to do anything
Except make this mess new

How long does it take to eat?
To wash and then to dress?
I give myself 4 hours
The rest to clean this mess

But if it's 2 and I work at 4
Maybe I can if I hurry
It seems the only time I have
Is the time I left to worry

Chronophobia

The laws of time are written so clearly
It goes on forever without stopping
The beauty of time deceives me as always
And I forget the meaning of the ticking

I tore apart the pretty picture painted in front of
me
And saw what lay underneath all this time
You know, even if I close my eyes, it will still be
there

I never liked the thought that this time keeps on
marching on
I don't care at all for the concept of eternity
These bitter words and hateful roars don't
accomplish anything
They've only left painful scars, and still time
won't stop

Why is the moon still waxing and waning?
Why does the sun still set every day?
I can hear that warped noise so close to me
No matter what, it keeps on ticking

I hide away and hope that nothing will find me

But still time will never know any bounds
I just want that horrible ticking to stop ringing in
my ears

Don't touch me, don't come near me, but still
time keeps marching on
I'm begging you, please kill me, I don't want
eternity
Why is it that the thing I most desperately don't
want to see
Is the only thing that will bleed under my closed
eyes?

If time could only stop for a moment
Then I would be able to breathe out my lament
But there is only the unstopping memory
That someone had violated me with

I hate everything about time that won't stop for
anyone
I never cared about the thought of existence
outside of me
The ticking and tocking of clocks that I've
broken
Please, just stop it now, and let me escape from
it

Control

Hello there, do you have a moment?
Just a second, if you like
I have something to sell to you
The name we haven't quite got right

We have this new device,
Sold to none before,
That can skip through time
When life is a bore

Now this device
Isn't hard to use
There's only one button
And it's your choice to choose

It takes your perception of time
(Or what we infer)
And makes what once felt long
Into a mere blur

There's no need to fret
About a start or stop
You hold down the button
Release when you ought

The time that you would rather
Be asleep than awake
Can feel like a second
It's a promise we make

Why not give it a try?
Hold in your hand like this
Skip ahead one hour
One hour won't be missed

Don't you like how it feels?
Now imagine all that can be done
Don't worry about the price
This is all in good fun

How about a trial run?
So if you don't like
A return can be made
I know it's only right

You say your job is boring?
Mindless, I get the gist
Just press the button firmly
And skip the entire shift

It's only eight hours
What would you miss?
Just hold down the button
And try to enjoy this

Nightmares you say?
You would rather stay awake?
Use this simple device
How many hours would that make?

Just skip it all entirely
Trust in me, I know
There's plenty to see in life
So many places to go

So skip all these things in life
Just press the button, okay?
Your mind is overwhelmed
There's too much to do today

All you do on your down time
Is read or watch TV?
You aren't doing anything of importance
So skip until there's something to see

You skipped over something you didn't mean?
Come on, get in line
I'm sorry, that wasn't professional
Just be careful next time

This product mimics time
So no, we can't go back

Time can only move forward
2nd chances are what we lack

You're asking what you should skip
How should I know? I'm not you
Skip it all if you'd like
That's what I would do

Think about it for a second
What is it you're waiting for?
You're living for the weekends
Then choose to stay indoors

So give it up and hold it down
Press the button and you'll see
Even if you skipped it all
There's nothing you'd be missing

Hello there, do you have a moment?
Just a second, if you like
I have something to sell to you
We call it your life

Swallow

I got a paper cut
And instinctually put my finger in my mouth
To suck the wound

And then I got a hangnail
And I imagined what it would be like
For the skin to never break
And it peels up and up and up

Nerve endings stinging
I unravel

And I consume

Blood in the mouth
Blood in the teeth
I chew holes
Through my cheeks

And I cut a piece of my ear
And put it with the blood
To stop the ringing
And swallow

I reach my fingers
Up under my ribcage
And quickly pull out
To break a piece off

And down my throat it goes
Back to where it started
But rather
Inside

I take a needle
And poke through my belly button
Pressure released
And my intestines come exploding out

And the pain is so great
But my hunger pains more
So I take a bite
and then another

my hands are slippery from my insides
coming out
but I pull and cry
and reach the end

so I grab and tear
up to my stomach

and the blood and bile
is sickening to see
but I eat more

I want nothing left

Where will I go
When I swallow it all?

Me

Simply stating a sentence
Almost always never amounts to anything
Restatement rarely reflects my reasoning
And things have to look and sound pretty to
Have it mean anything to you

Cowardice

I want to say the words inside my head
Those little simple words, I've dared not said
Spinning and swirling, I've hit a wall
But you just asked me if 'that was all?'

If I weren't here, it won't change a thing
The world will just keep turning

If it's alright, then I'm fine
It doesn't hurt at all
I'll just continue to be a coward
If it's alright, then I'm fine
I'll just forget it all
I'll learn to choke it down just like a desert

TBD

If I wrote about my life
Where would I begin?
Would it be best in medias res,
Or should I start at the end?

If I wrote about my life
How many drafts would there be?
Would it be best to never finish,
Or publish after three?

There would need to be a plot
A beginning, a middle, an end
For some spice, I'll add a twist
The protagonist ends up dead

If I wrote about my life
What characters would we see?
We know the heroine, and the comic relief,
But the villain would be me

Growing Pains

31

Everyone grew up

And forgot all about me